Sanjeev Kapoor's

Tawa-H

Recipes

In association with Alyona Kapoor

PopulaR
prakashan

www.popularprakashan.com

Published by
POPULAR PRAKASHAN PVT. LTD.
301, Mahalaxmi Chambers
22, Bhulabhai Desai Road
Mumbai - 400 026
for KHANA KHAZANA PUBLICATIONS PVT. LTD.

(4328)
ISBN: 978-81-7991-580-6

Design: Anjali Sawant
Typesetting: Satyavan Rane

PRINTED IN INDIA
by Saurabh Printers Pvt. Ltd.
A-16, Sector 4, Noida

AUTHOR'S NOTE

*N*o Indian kitchen is complete without a *handi* or a *tawa*.

The *handi* with its narrow mouth, deep and bulbous body and thick bottom is used for everything from boiling water to cooking curries and *biryani*. The *handi* however is best used for slow (*dum*) cooking over low heat, producing soft, succulent meats, thick, creamy *dal* and aromatic *biryani*, with all their exotic flavours sealed in its depth. One of the most delightful culinary experiences is to inhale the perfumed vapours released from the contents of a freshly opened sealed *handi*. The earthenware *handi* has a special place in traditional kitchens. The flavours of damp earth that leach into the food give it a rustic touch that is hard to replicate.

And what would one do without a *tawa*! This multipurpose kitchen utensil is used to cook *roti* and *paranthe*, toast spices, shallow-fry *tikki* or barbecue *kababs*. The street food vendor's friend, *tawa* produces *dosai*, *pav-bhaji* and *ragda-pattice* at the scrape and clang of a metal *palta*. A cousin of the griddle, the thick cast-iron *tawa* with a shallow concave centre, tempers with age and use, forming its own non-stick coating to rival more modern *avatars*.

The recipes in this book celebrate these two stalwarts of our kitchens. Long may they continue to reign!

Happy cooking!

CONTENTS

TAWA

HANDI

GLOSSARY

Tawa Paneer Chaat

Ingredients

500 grams cottage cheese, cut into ½-inch pieces

Crisp puffed *puri* (as for *paani puri*)

3 tablespoons oil

2 large onions, chopped

1 teaspoon ginger paste

1 teaspoon garlic paste

3-4 green chillies, seeded and chopped

¾ cup tomato purée

3-4 tablespoons *pav bhaji masala*

Salt to taste

½ tablespoon *chaat masala*

2-3 tablespoons chopped fresh coriander

Method

1. Heat the oil on a *tawa*; add the onions and sauté till brown. Add the ginger paste and garlic paste and continue to sauté for a few minutes.

2. Add a little water and continue to sauté for one minute. Add the green chillies and sauté for another minute.

3. Add the tomato purée, *pav bhaji masala*, salt and *chaat masala* and continue to cook over low heat till the oil separates from the *masala*.

4. Add the cottage cheese and half the chopped coriander and stir gently to mix. Check seasoning and cook over low heat for two minutes.

5. Make a hole in each *puri* and stuff with the cottage cheese mixture. Serve, garnished with the remaining chopped coriander.

Hara Bhara Paneer Tikka

Ingredients

300 grams cottage cheese, cut into
1½-inch squares

2 bunches (120 grams) fresh coriander,
roughly chopped

1 bunch (60 grams) fresh mint,
roughly chopped

4 green chillies, roughly chopped

10 garlic cloves, roughly chopped

1 cup yogurt

3 tablespoons gram flour

Salt to taste

1 teaspoon *chaat masala*

½ teaspoon *garam masala* powder

1 tablespoon lemon juice

1 tablespoon oil

Method

1. Coarsely grind the chopped coriander
   and mint, green chillies and garlic.
   Transfer to a bowl, add the yogurt,
   gram flour, salt, *chaat masala*, *garam
   masala* powder and lemon juice and
   mix well.

2. Stir in the oil, add the cottage cheese
   and mix well so that all the pieces are
   well-coated with the mixture.

3. Set aside to marinate for about half an hour.

4. Heat a *tawa*. Thread the cottage cheese pieces one-inch apart onto skewers and grill turning from time to time, for about fifteen minutes, or till evenly cooked on all sides.

5. Serve hot with onion rings and lemon wedges.

Green Pea and Coconut Tikki

Ingredients

1 cup shelled green peas, boiled and mashed slightly

½ cup grated coconut

4 large potatoes, boiled and mashed

Salt to taste

2 tablespoons oil + for shallow-frying

2 teaspoons cumin seeds

1 inch ginger, finely chopped

3 green chillies, finely chopped

A pinch of asafoetida

1 teaspoon lemon juice

½ cup fresh coriander, finely chopped

Green Chutney (see below), as required

Method

1. Knead the mashed potatoes with salt till smooth.

2. Heat two tablespoons of oil in a pan; add the cumin seeds, asafoetida, chopped ginger and green chillies, the boiled green peas and a little salt. Stir-fry for two to three minutes. Add a little lemon juice and spread out on a plate to cool.

3. Add the chopped coriander and grated coconut and mix.

4. Place a portion of mashed potato on the moistened palm of one hand; make a dent in the centre, fill it with the pea and coconut mixture and bring in the edges to enclose the stuffing. Press gently and roll the edges to smoothen the sides.

5. Place the *tikki* in the refrigerator for five to seven minutes.

6. Heat a little oil on a *tawa* and shallow-fry the *tikki* on low heat until light brown and crisp.

7. Serve hot with green chutney.

| Green Chutney |

Grind together 1 cup fresh coriander, ½ cup fresh mint, 2-3 green chillies, black salt to taste, ¼ teaspoon sugar and 1 tablespoon lemon juice to a smooth paste using a little water if required.

Pav Bhaji Roll-Ups

Ingredients

4 tortillas

8 lettuce leaves

Pav Bhaji

3 tablespoons oil

2 medium onions, chopped

3-4 green chillies, chopped

2 teaspoons ginger paste

2 teaspoons garlic paste

4 medium tomatoes, chopped

1 medium green capsicum, chopped

¼ cup shelled green peas, boiled
and mashed lightly

¼ small cauliflower, grated

4 medium potatoes, boiled and grated

1½ tablespoons *pav bhaji masala*

Salt to taste

2 tablespoons chopped fresh coriander

Onion-Cheese Mixture

1 large onion, sliced

2 large tomatoes, seeded and sliced

1 cup grated processed cheese

½ teaspoon red chilli powder

Method

1. To make the *pav bhaji*, heat the oil on a large *tawa* and add three-fourth of the onions; sauté till light brown. Add the green chillies, ginger paste and garlic paste and sauté for half a minute.

2. Add half the tomatoes and cook over medium heat, stirring continuously, for three to four minutes, or till the oil separates from the *masala*.

3. Add the capsicum, peas, cauliflower, potatoes and one and a half cups of water. Bring to a boil and simmer for ten minutes, pressing with the back of the ladle a few times, till all the vegetables are completely mashed.

4. Add the *pav bhaji masala*, salt and the remaining tomatoes. Cook over medium heat for two minutes, stirring continuously.

5. At this point you can transfer the *bhaji* to a *kadai* and simmer for five to ten minutes, stirring often, till all the moisture evaporates and the *bhaji* is quite dry.

6. Add the chopped coriander and mix. Transfer to a bowl and set aside.

7. Mix all the ingredients for the onion-cheese mixture together. Heat a *tawa* and lightly warm each tortilla on both sides.

8. Place a warmed tortilla on a square piece of aluminium foil. Spread one-fourth of the *bhaji* over the tortilla and generously sprinkle one-fourth of the onion-cheese mixture over it.

9. Place two lettuce leaves at one end of the tortilla and roll up tightly. Wrap in the foil. Serve hot.

— Chef's Tip —

You can, of course, serve the *bhaji* with buttered *pav* toasted on the *tawa* to make the original Mumbai *pav-bhaji*!

17

Ragda Pattice

Ingredients

1¼ cups dried white peas

4 large potatoes, boiled and mashed

¼ teaspoon turmeric powder

A pinch of asafoetida

Salt to taste

2 tablespoons cornflour

2-3 green chillies, chopped

Oil for shallow-frying

Green Chutney (page 13)

Date And Tamarind (see below)

2 medium onions, chopped

2 teaspoons *chaat masala*

2 tablespoons chopped fresh coriander

Method

1. Soak the dried peas in three cups of water overnight, or for at least six hours.

2. Drain and boil in three to four cups of water with the turmeric powder, asafoetida and salt till soft. Mash the peas slightly. Add a little water if the gravy is too thick and simmer for ten minutes. Keep the *ragda* hot.

3. For the *pattice* add the cornflour, green chillies and salt to the potatoes and mix well. Divide into eight equal portions and shape into balls. Flatten slightly.

4. Heat a little oil on a *tawa* and fry the *pattice* gently on both sides over medium heat till evenly browned. Keep warm.

5. For each serving, place two *pattice* on a plate and pour some *ragda* over.

6. Drizzle with green chutney and date and tamarind chutney; sprinkle onions, *chaat masala* and chopped coriander on top. Serve immediately.

| Date and Tamarind Chutney |

Wash, stone and chop 15-20 dates. Dry-roast 2 teaspoons cumin seeds and
¼ teaspoon fennel seeds. Cool and grind to a powder. Cook dates,
1 cup tamarind pulp, cumin and fennel powder, ½ cup jaggery,
2 teaspoons red chilli powder, 1 teaspoon dried ginger powder,
black salt, salt and four cups of water till thick.

Cheeley Poode

Ingredients

2 cups gram flour

½ cup chopped fresh fenugreek

Salt to taste

¼ teaspoon turmeric powder

1 teaspoon red chilli powder

½ teaspoon *chaat masala* powder

1 tablespoon lemon juice

1 medium onion, chopped

Oil for shallow-frying

1 cup grated cottage cheese

½ cup grated cheese

1 teaspoon red chilli powder

Method

1. Combine the gram flour, chopped fenugreek, salt, turmeric powder, chilli powder, *chaat masala* powder, lemon juice and onion in a bowl. Stir in three-fourth cup of water to make a moderately thick batter.

2. Heat a *tawa* and add a little oil. Pour a ladleful of batter and spread it slightly over the *tawa*. Cook over low heat till the *cheeley* is cooked on one side. Drizzle some oil around the sides and over the top.

3. Place some grated cottage cheese in the centre of the *cheeley*. Sprinkle with grated cheese and chilli powder.

4. Fold the two sides over the stuffing and serve hot.

Image on inside front cover.

Set Dosa

Ingredients

2 cups rice

½ teaspoon fenugreek seeds

1 cup beaten rice

1 cup yogurt

Salt to taste

Oil, as required

Method

1. Wash and soak the rice and fenugreek seeds in four cups of warm water for about two hours. Soak the beaten rice in a little water for about five minutes.

2. Grind the rice and fenugreek seeds along with the beaten rice and salt into a smooth, thick batter. Add the yogurt and salt and mix well.

3. Keep the batter in a warm place to ferment overnight. Heat a *tawa* and grease it. For each *dosa*, pour a ladleful of batter onto the *tawa*, but do not spread it. The batter will set in a thick round.

4. Drizzle a little oil all around the *dosa* and cover it with a lid. Cook till the underside is done and very light brown. Serve hot with chutney or *sambhar*.

— Chef's Tip —

For added flavour, grind green chillies and ginger with the rest of the ingredients.

Chicken Seekh Kabab

Ingredients

500 grams finely minced chicken

1-2 green chillies, finely chopped

1 medium onion, finely chopped

1 inch ginger, finely chopped

4 garlic cloves, finely chopped

2 tablespoons finely chopped
cashew nuts

1 teaspoon *chaat masala*

1 teaspoon *garam masala* powder

1 teaspoon white pepper powder

2 tablespoons chopped fresh coriander

1 tablespoon lemon juice

Salt to taste

Oil, as required

2 tablespoons butter

Method

1. In a bowl, mix together the minced
   chicken, green chillies, onion, ginger,
   garlic, cashew nuts, *chaat masala*,
   garam masala powder, white pepper
   powder, chopped coriander, lemon
   juice and salt.

2. Alternatively, you can use boneless
   chicken and grind it together with
   the green chillies, onion, ginger and

garlic. Add the remaining ingredients and mix.

3. Heat a *tawa* and drizzle some oil on it. Wet your hands, take a little chicken mixture and shape it around a satay stick, pressing the mixture firmly.

4. Place the *seekh kababs* on the *tawa*. Cook, turning from time to time, so that the *kababs* cook evenly all around. Baste with butter at regular intervals.

5. Serve hot.

— Chef's Tip —
For best results, use minced chicken breast.

Sabudana Thalipeeth

Ingredients

1 cup sago, soaked

2 medium potatoes, boiled, peeled and mashed

2-3 green chillies, chopped

¼ teaspoon red chilli powder

½ cup crushed roasted peanuts

2 tablespoons chopped fresh coriander

1 tablespoon cumin seeds

Salt to taste

Oil for greasing

4-5 teaspoons ghee

Method

1. Mix together the sago, mashed potatoes, green chillies, chilli powder, roasted peanuts, chopped coriander, cumin seeds and salt.

2. Divide the mixture into four portions and form each portion into a ball.

3. Grease a thick plastic or polythene sheet with a little oil and place the sago ball on it. Flatten the ball with moistened or greased fingers into a thick round.

4. Heat a *tawa* and add a teaspoon of ghee. Transfer the *thalipeeth* to the *tawa* by gently turning the *thalipeeth* out on to the *tawa* and peeling the plastic off.

5. Cook, spreading both sides with ghee till light golden brown.

6. Serve hot with chutney.

— Chef's Tip —

Use a cut open washed plastic milk pouch on which to roll out the *thalipeeth*.

Yakitori Chicken with Spring Onions

Ingredients

500 grams chicken thigh or breast
   pieces, cut into 1-inch cubes

4 spring onions, halved

1 large red capsicum, cut into
   1-inch pieces

4 button mushrooms, halved

8 fresh shiitake mushrooms

2 tablespoons oil

8 satay sticks, soaked in water for
   a few minutes

Sauce

½ cup sake

½ cup Japanese soy sauce

2 tablespoons sugar

Salt to taste

½ teaspoon black pepper powder

Method

1. Halve the mushrooms and spring
   onions. To make the sauce, pour
   the sake into a small pan; add the
   soy sauce and sugar and bring the
   mixture to a boil. Add the salt and
   pepper powder and mix.

2. Lower the heat and simmer, uncovered, over medium heat until the sauce reduces to one-third. Cool.

3. Take a satay stick and thread onto it a spring onion half, two chicken cubes, a piece of red capsicum, half a button mushroom, a shiitake mushroom, two more chicken cubes and finally a piece of red capsicum. Leave a little space between each ingredient to allow even cooking. Prepare the remaining satay sticks in the same way.

4. Heat one tablespoon oil on a *tawa*. Place four satay sticks at a time on it and cook, turning and brushing with the sauce occasionally, until browned all over and cooked through.

5. Serve the yakitori sprinkled with remaining sauce.

Baida Roti

Ingredients

Roti

1 cup refined flour

Salt to taste

1 tablespoon oil

$1/8$ teaspoon baking powder

1 egg

1 cup minced mutton

2 green chillies, chopped

Salt to taste

¼ teaspoon *garam masala* powder

1 tablespoon chopped fresh coriander

Filling

8 eggs

1 tablespoon oil + for shallow-frying

1 medium onion, minced

Method

1. Mix together the refined flour, salt, oil, baking powder and egg. Add one-fourth cup of water and knead into a soft dough.

2. Divide the dough into four equal portions and shape into balls. Cover the dough with a damp cloth and set aside for a few minutes.

3. For the filling, heat one tablespoon of oil in a pan; add the onion and sauté till light brown. Add the minced mutton, green chillies and salt and cook over medium heat till the mince is cooked and completely dry. Add the *garam masala* powder and chopped coriander and mix well. Beat the eggs well.

4. Roll out each ball of dough into an eight-inch square *roti*.

5. Heat a non-stick pan and place the *roti* on it. Place some mince *masala* in the centre and pour two tablespoons of beaten egg over. Fold in the sides to make a square package.

6. Pour some more beaten egg over and drizzle oil around the stuffed *roti*. Slowly turn the stuffed *roti* over and pour a little more beaten egg so that the *roti* is covered with egg on all sides. Gently fry over low heat till both sides are golden and crisp.

7. Serve hot with Green Chutney (page 13).

Mutton Frankies

Ingredients

350 grams boneless mutton, cut into
  ½-inch thin pieces
1½ cups refined flour
2 tablespoons oil + for shallow-frying
3 large onions
2 teaspoons ginger paste
2 teaspoons garlic paste
Salt to taste
2 teaspoons coriander powder
½ teaspoon turmeric powder
2 teaspoons red chilli powder
2 large tomatoes, chopped
2 tablespoons fresh coriander,
  finely chopped

½ teaspoon *garam masala* powder
3 eggs, beaten
4 teaspoons chilli vinegar

Method

1. Roughly chop two onions and slice
   the remaining one.

2. Mix the refined flour and salt in a
   bowl. Add sufficient water and knead
   into a soft dough.

3. Heat two tablespoons of oil in a
   pressure cooker. Add the roughly
   chopped onion and sauté for two

minutes. Add the ginger paste and garlic paste and continue to sauté for another minute.

4. Add the mutton and sauté for two to three minutes. Add the salt, coriander powder, turmeric powder and chilli powder and mix well.

5. Add the tomatoes and sauté for two or three minutes. Add a quarter cup of water. When the mixture comes to a boil, secure the lid of the pressure cooker and cook till the pressure is released five or six times (five or six whistles).

6. Remove the lid when the pressure has reduced completely. Stir in the fresh

coriander and *garam masala* powder and cook till the mixture is dry.

7. Divide the dough into eight equal portions and roll out into *roti*. Cook each *roti*, on a hot *tawa* till almost done.

8. Pour some beaten egg over the *roti* and cook till set. Turn over to cook the other side.

9. Place the *roti*, egg side up, on a serving plate. Place some of the mutton mixture at one end. Sprinkle some onion over the mutton. Drizzle some chilli vinegar and roll up firmly. Serve immediately.

Roti Prata with Brinjal Curry

Ingredients

Roti Prata

2 cups refined flour

Salt to taste

1 teaspoon powdered sugar

1 cup oil + for shallow-frying

Brinjal Curry

3 medium brinjals, cubed

Salt to taste

6 tablespoons coconut powder

2 tablespoons oil

2 medium onions, sliced

2½ teaspoons curry powder

1 cup Vegetable Stock

½ teaspoon red chilli powder

2 medium potatoes, boiled and cubed

Method

1. For the dough, place the refined flour, salt and powdered sugar in a bowl. Add sufficient water and knead into a very soft dough.

2. Add ten tablespoons of oil and knead again. Cover the dough with a damp cloth and set aside for two hours.

3. For the curry, soak the brinjal cubes in salted water. Place the brinjals in a

microwave-safe bowl with water and cook in the microwave oven on HIGH (100%) for three minutes.

4. Mix the coconut powder with one cup of water to make coconut milk.

5. Heat the oil in a pan; add the onions and sauté till golden brown. Add the curry powder and mix. Stir in the vegetable stock. Add the chilli powder and cook for two to three minutes.

6. Add the potatoes, brinjals and salt. Stir and add the coconut milk. Bring the mixture to a boil, lower the heat and simmer for five minutes.

7. Divide the dough into eight equal portions and shape into balls. Spread each ball out with your hand. Brush one tablespoon of oil over the dough and fold over twice. Rest the dough for five minutes.

8. Roll out again and brush with one tablespoon of oil. Fold and rest again for five minutes. Roll each one out into a square *parantha*.

9. Heat a *tawa*. Place a *parantha* on it and cook over high heat. Turn and brush with half a tablespoon of oil and fry till golden brown. Turn over again, brush with half a tablespoon of oil and fry till the other side turns golden brown as well. Remove from the *tawa* and crush lightly. Serve hot with the brinjal curry.

Paneer Kulcha

Ingredients

Kulcha Dough

2 cups refined flour

½ teaspoon baking powder

¼ teaspoon soda bicarbonate

½ teaspoon salt

1 teaspoon sugar

½ cup milk

1 tablespoon yogurt

3 tablespoons oil

Melted pure ghee, as required

Filling

200 grams cottage cheese, grated

2 green chillies, chopped

2 tablespoons chopped fresh coriander

Salt to taste

Method

1. Sift the flour with the baking powder, soda bicarbonate and salt into a bowl. Add the sugar, milk, yogurt and one-fourth cup of water. Knead well into a medium-soft dough.

2. Spread a little oil on the dough, cover with a damp cloth and set aside for one hour.

3. Divide the dough into four equal portions and shape into balls.

4. For the filling, place the cottage cheese in a bowl; add the green chillies, coriander and salt and mix well. Divide into four equal portions.

5. Place the balls of dough on a lightly floured worktop and flatten slightly.

Place a portion of the cottage cheese filling in the centre of each one, gather the edges together and pinch to seal the filling. Cover with a damp cloth and set aside for five minutes.

6. Flatten each ball between your palms into a nine-inch round *kulcha*.

7. Heat a *tawa* and cook the *kulcha* till both sides are evenly cooked.

8. Remove from heat, brush with the melted ghee and serve hot.

Note: You can also bake the *kulcha* in a moderately hot oven for about fifteen minutes

Tawa Vegetables

Ingredients

4 small brinjals, slit into four

2 bitter gourds, halved, cored, and cut into four

4 medium pointed gourds, slit into four

8 ivy gourds, slit into four

8 baby potatoes, boiled and peeled

8 shallots

8 fresh button mushrooms, quartered

8 ladies' fingers, slit into four

6 tablespoons oil + for deep-frying

4 medium onions, chopped

3 inches ginger, chopped

6-8 green chillies, seeded and chopped

8 teaspoons *pav bhaji masala*

Salt to taste

16 tablespoons tomato purée

4 tablespoons fresh chopped coriander

Method

1. Heat the oil in a *kadai* and deep-fry the brinjals and bitter gourds till lightly browned. Drain on absorbent paper.

2. Add the both types of gourds to the same oil and deep-fry till lightly browned. Drain on absorbent paper.

3. Add the baby potatoes, shallots, mushrooms and ladies' fingers one after the other. Deep-fry and drain on absorbent paper.

4. Heat a *tawa*. Arrange the fried vegetables around the edge of the *tawa*.

5. For each serving, heat one tablespoon of oil, add a quarter of the chopped onions and sauté till brown. Add a quarter of the ginger and continue to sauté.

6. Add a little water to the *tawa* and stir. Add a quarter of the green chillies and sauté for a few seconds.

7. Add a quarter of each vegetable to the *masala*. Add two teaspoons of *pav bhaji masala*, salt, four tablespoons of tomato purée and a little water and mix well. Cook for three to four minutes and serve hot. Repeat for the remaining three serving.

8. Garnish with chopped coriander and serve hot.

Mooli Bajra Roti

Ingredients

3 medium radishes, grated

2 cups millet flour + for dusting

Salt to taste

1 small onion, finely chopped

2 green chillies, finely chopped

1 teaspoon red chilli powder

1 teaspoon ginger paste

1 teaspoon dried mango powder

½ teaspoon *garam masala* powder

2 tablespoons finely chopped coriander

Ghee for shallow-frying

Method

1. Mix some salt into the grated radish and set aside for half an hour. Squeeze tightly to remove excess moisture.

2. In a deep bowl, mix together the radish, millet flour, onion, green chillies, chilli powder, ginger paste, dried mango powder, *garam masala* powder, chopped coriander and salt thoroughly. Add sufficient warm water and knead into a dough.

3. Divide the dough into eight equal portions and roll into balls. Lightly dust each ball with flour, place on a plastic sheet and pat with your fingers into a thick *roti*.

4. Heat a *tawa* and place the *roti* on it. Cook for a while, then flip the *roti* over and drizzle some ghee all around. till both sides are cooked and golden brown. Serve hot with a dollop of ghee.

5. Flip the *roti* over again and drizzle some more ghee all around and cook

— Chef's Tip —

Do not rest the dough as the radish will release water and make the dough sticky.

Lasun and Rice Thepla

Ingredients

2 cups wholewheat flour

1 tablespoon garlic paste

2 tablespoons fresh green garlic, chopped (optional)

1 cup leftover cooked rice, mashed

½ teaspoon turmeric powder

1 teaspoon red chilli powder

Salt to taste

2 tablespoons chopped fresh coriander

4 tablespoons oil + for shallow-frying

Method

1. Place the wholewheat flour, garlic paste, fresh green garlic, mashed rice, turmeric powder, chilli powder, salt and chopped coriander in a bowl.

2. Mix in four tablespoons of oil and knead with enough water into a medium soft dough.

3. Divide into twelve portions and roll each one out thinly into a five-inch round *thepla*.

4. Heat a *tawa* and cook the *thepla* on both sides drizzling a little oil around.

5. Serve hot with pickle or yogurt.

Koki

Ingredients

2½ cups wholewheat flour

2 small onions, roughly chopped

2-3 green chillies, finely chopped

2 tablespoons fresh coriander, chopped

Salt to taste

1 tablespoon ghee + for shallow-frying

4 tablespoons fresh cream

Method

1. Mix together the flour, chopped onions, green chillies, chopped coriander, salt, ghee and cream in a bowl. Add enough water to make a stiff dough. Cover and rest the dough for about fifteen minutes.

2. Divide the dough into eight equal portions, larger than that needed to make a *parantha*. Pat with your fingers into a thick round.

3. Heat a *tawa*, place a *koki* on it and cook on both sides. Brush with pure ghee and cook till both sides are light golden in colour. Serve hot.

Mushroom, Babycorn and Paneer Tawa Masala

Ingredients

8-10 fresh button mushrooms, halved

8-10 ears of babycorn, halved and boiled

400 grams cottage cheese, cut into 1½-inch cubes

10 baby potatoes, parboiled

10-15 shallots

5 teaspoons + 3 tablespoons oil

2 large onions, chopped

1½ inches ginger, chopped

3-4 green chillies, chopped

½ teaspoon coriander power

½ teaspoon red chilli powder

4 teaspoons *garam masala* powder

Salt to taste

8 tablespoons tomato purée

1 tablespoon lemon juice

2 tablespoons chopped fresh coriander

Method

1. Sauté the mushrooms, babycorn, cottage cheese, baby potatoes and shallots separately in one teaspoon of oil each, sprinkling a little salt as you sauté. Drain and set aside.

2. Heat three tablespoons of oil on a *tawa*; add the onions and sauté till brown.

3. Add the ginger and continue to sauté. Add a little water and cook for a few minutes.

4. Place the sautéed cottage cheese and vegetables around the edge of the *tawa*.

5. Add the green chillies to the onion mixture and continue to sauté.

6. Draw the vegetables and cottage cheese into the *masala* at the centre of the *tawa*.

7. Add the coriander powder, chilli powder, *garam masala* powder, salt, tomato purée and half a cup of water and mix well.

8. Cook for three or four minutes, add the lemon juice and mix well.

9. Garnish with the chopped coriander and serve hot.

Murgh Missi Roti

Ingredients

1½ cups minced chicken

1 cup wholewheat flour

1 cup gram flour

Salt to taste

1 teaspoon turmeric powder

1 teaspoon *chaat masala*

4 green chillies, chopped

1 tablespoon dried pomegranate seeds

1 medium onion, finely chopped

2 tablespoons chopped fresh coriander

1 egg

1 tablespoon oil + for shallow-frying

Method

1. Mix the wholewheat flour, gram flour, salt, turmeric powder, *chaat masala*, green chillies, dried pomegranate seeds, onion, fresh coriander, minced chicken and egg.

2. Add a little oil and just enough water to knead into a soft dough. Divide the dough into equal portions.

3. Grease your palms and roll the portions into balls.

4. Heat a *tawa*. Roll each ball in some flour and roll out into a thick *roti*.

5. Place on the hot *tawa* and cook over medium heat on both sides.

6. Drizzle some oil around the *roti* and when one side turns golden brown, flip it over and drizzle some more oil, cooking the other side till golden brown. Serve immediately.

7. Alternatively, apply a little oil to the dough balls and grease the worktop. With greased fingers, gently pat each ball of dough into a thickish *roti* and cook on the *tawa* as above.

Dum Paneer Mitti Handi

Ingredients

400 grams creamy cottage cheese, cut into 1-inch cubes

2 tablespoons oil

2 bay leaves

2 green cardamoms

2 cloves

¾ inch cinnamon

1 teaspoon ginger paste

1 teaspoon garlic paste

¾ teaspoon green chilli paste

½ cup browned onion paste

¾ teaspoon cumin powder

1½ tablespoons coriander powder

6-8 black peppercorns, crushed

Salt to taste

¾ cup yogurt, whisked

½ cup fresh cream

A generous pinch of saffron

3 green cardamoms, crushed

¾ tablespoon garam masala powder

3 tablespoons finely chopped fresh coriander

1½ tablespoons finely chopped fresh mint

A few rose petals

1½ teaspoons rose water

Wholewheat dough to seal the pan

Method

1. Preheat an oven to 180°C/350°F/ Gas Mark 4.

2. Heat the oil in a pan; add the bay leaves, cardamoms, cloves and cinnamon and sauté till fragrant. Add the ginger paste, garlic paste and green chilli paste and mix well. Add the browned onion paste and mix.

3. Stir in one cup of water and cook for two minutes. Add the cumin powder, coriander powder, crushed peppercorns and salt and sauté for one minute. Add the yogurt and mix well.

4. Add the cottage cheese to the gravy and cook over medium heat. Stir in the fresh cream and the saffron.

5. Transfer the mixture to a *mitti ki handi*. Gently stir in the crushed cardamoms, *garam masala* powder, chopped coriander and mint, rose petals and rose water. Cover with the lid and seal the edges with wholewheat dough .

6. Place the *handi* in the oven and cook for ten to fifteen minutes. Break open the seal and serve hot.

Thikri Ki Dal

Ingredient

1½ cups split red lentils

Salt to taste

½ tablespoon red chilli powder

¼ tablespoon turmeric powder

6 tablespoons pure ghee

1 large onion, sliced

4 green chillies, broken in half

2 tablespoons chopped fresh coriander

1 teaspoon cumin seeds

4-5 dried red chillies

8-10 garlic cloves, chopped

¼ teaspoon fenugreek seeds

25 curry leaves

2 three-inch pieces of earthenware
(thikri)

2 tablespoons lemon juice

Method

1. Bring the lentils, salt and five cups of water to a boil in a *handi*. Remove the scum and add the chilli powder and turmeric powder. When half-cooked,

add one tablespoon of ghee. Cook over low heat till the lentils are very soft; mash the lentils with the back of a ladle.

2. Heat three tablespoons of ghee in a pan and sauté the onion till golden brown.

3. Add to the lentils with the green chillies and chopped coriander and cook for five minutes over low heat.

4. Heat the remaining ghee in a pan; add the cumin seeds, red chillies,

garlic, fenugreek seeds and curry leaves.

5. When the chillies begin to darken, pour the spices over the lentils and cover immediately to trap the flavours.

6. Wash the *thikri*. Heat over burning charcoal or a flame till red hot. Place in the *handi* with the lentils and cover the pan immediately.

7. Just before serving, remove the *thikri* and discard. Stir in the lemon juice and serve at once.

Diwani Handi

Ingredients

3 medium potatoes, peeled and cut into
½-inch cubes

3 medium carrots, cut into ½-inch cubes

10-12 French beans, cut diagonally

10-12 broad beans, cut diagonally

4-6 small brinjals, slit

½ cup green peas

3 tablespoons oil

2 medium onions, sliced

2-3 green chillies, seeded and chopped

1 tablespoon ginger paste

1 tablespoon garlic paste

1 teaspoon red chilli powder

½ teaspoon turmeric powder

Salt to taste

2 tablespoons yogurt

½ bunch (150 grams) fresh
    fenugreek, chopped

2 tablespoons chopped fresh coriander

½ teaspoon *garam masala* powder

Method

1. Heat the oil in a *handi*; add the onions and sauté till light brown. Add the green chillies, ginger paste and garlic paste and sauté for one minute. Add the chilli powder, turmeric powder and salt and mix well. Add the yogurt and stir-fry for two or three minutes.

2. Add all the vegetables and simmer, covered, till tender. Add the chopped fenugreek and coriander and the *garam masala* powder, stir and cook for three or four minutes.

3. Serve hot with any Indian bread.

Dum Paneer Kali Mirch

Ingredients

400 grams creamy cottage cheese,
  cut into 1-inch cubes
1 tablespoon crushed peppercorns
1 inch ginger
4-5 garlic cloves
2-3 green chillies
Oil for deep-frying
2 medium onions, finely sliced
2 tablespoons pure ghee
2 bay leaves
1 inch cinnamon
3-4 green cardamoms
3-4 cloves

1 cup yogurt, whisked
2 tablespoons coriander powder
1 teaspoon cumin powder
Salt to taste
½ cup fresh coriander, finely chopped
¼ cup fresh mint, finely chopped
½ cup fresh cream
1 teaspoon *garam masala* powder

Method

1. Preheat an oven to 200°C/400°F/
   Gas Mark 6. Grind the ginger, garlic
   and green chillies to a fine paste.

2. Heat the oil in a *kadai* and deep-fry the sliced onions, till golden brown. Drain on absorbent paper and set aside to cool. Grind the fried onions with two tablespoons of water to a smooth paste.

3. Heat the ghee in a narrow-mouthed *handi*; add the bay leaves, cinnamon, cardamoms, and cloves and stir-fry for a few seconds. Add the ginger-garlic-green chilli paste and sauté over high heat for half a minute.

4. Add the brown onion paste, whisked yogurt, coriander powder, cumin powder and salt to taste. Stir well, add one cup of water and cook over high heat, stirring frequently, till the gravy comes to a boil.

5. Add the cottage cheese, chopped coriander and mint. Stir in the fresh cream and crushed peppercorns and sprinkle the *garam masala* powder.

6. Cover the *handi* with a tight-fitting lid and seal it using wholewheat flour dough or alternatively, seal it tightly with aluminium foil. Place the sealed *handi* in the oven and cook for ten to fifteen minutes. Open the *handi* just before serving.

— Chef's Tip —

You can also transfer the cottage cheese to four single-portion copper *handi* and proceed as above. Let the guests open their individual handi at the dining table to enjoy the delicate fragrance of *dum* cooking.

Dum Raan

Ingredients

1 whole (1 kg) leg of goat or lamb

250 grams yogurt

1 tablespoon lemon juice

Salt to taste

6 garlic cloves

2 inches ginger

¼ teaspoon asafoetida

8 black peppercorns

3 medium onions

½ tablespoon *garam masala* powder

4 tablespoons unripe papaya paste

½ cup oil

1 teaspoon red chilli powder

1 teaspoon dried ginger powder

100 grams *khoya/mawa*

1 teaspoon sugar

Method

1. Trim the leg of lamb and rub a mixture of the yogurt, lemon juice and salt all over it; leave to marinate for fifteen minutes.

2. Grind together the garlic, ginger, asafoetida, peppercorns and onions to a smooth paste. Add the *garam masala* powder and rub the mixture

over the leg of lamb along with the papaya paste. Prick the leg of lamb all over with a fork. Leave to marinate for two to three hours, preferably in a refrigerator.

3. Heat the oil in a large *handi* or heavy-bottomed pan over low heat. Place the leg of lamb, chilli powder, ginger powder, *khoya* and sugar in the pan with three cups of water. Cover and cook over low heat turning the leg of lamb over occasionally so that it cooks evenly on all sides.

4. When the mutton is tender and the gravy is almost dry, take it out of the pan carefully and place on a serving dish. Serve hot.

— Chef's Tip —
Marinate the leg of lamb overnight, so that the meat cooks faster and remains tender.

Dum Ka Murgh

Ingredients

1 chicken (800 grams), cut into 8 pieces

2 one-inch fresh ginger, peeled and roughly chopped

6-8 garlic cloves, peeled and roughly chopped

3-4 green chillies, roughly chopped

15-20 almonds

4 tablespoons ghee + for deep-frying

2 medium onions, peeled and sliced

1½ cups yogurt

Salt to taste

2 bay leaves

1 tablespoon coriander powder

1 teaspoon cumin powder

¼ teaspoon mace powder

¼ teaspoon green cardamom powder

½ teaspoon black cardamom powder

¼ teaspoon cinnamon powder

½ cup fresh cream

Method

1. Grind together the ginger, garlic and green chillies to a paste. Soak the almonds in one cup of hot water for ten minutes; peel and grind to a fine paste. Heat sufficient ghee in a *kadai* and deep-fry the sliced onions till golden brown. Drain on absorbent paper. Cool and grind the fried onions to a fine paste.

2. Marinate the chicken in a mixture of the yogurt, ginger-garlic-green chilli paste and salt for two hours, preferably in a refrigerator.

3. Heat four tablespoons of ghee in a *handi*; add the bay leaves and sauté for a few seconds. Add the marinated chicken and cook till the gravy begins to boil. Stir in the coriander and cumin powders, browned onion paste and almond paste dissolved in half a cup of water.

4. Cover the *handi* with a tight-fitting lid or aluminium foil. Alternatively, seal the lid with wholewheat flour dough, so that the flavours and aroma are contained in the *handi* and do not escape. Cook over low heat till fragrant.

5. Uncover the *handi* and sprinkle with mace powder, green and black cardamom powders and cinnamon powder. Stir in the fresh cream. Serve hot.

— Chef's Tip —

It is believed, that if the *handi* is sealed with wholewheat flour dough, as soon as the dish is ready, the handi will give out an aroma which will beckon the person cooking the dish to give the finishing touches.

Chandi Korma

Ingredients

1 whole chicken (1 kg), cut into 12 pieces

3 tablespoons oil

3 medium onions, sliced

1 tablespoon ginger paste

1 tablespoon garlic paste

1 tablespoon green chilli paste

¼ cup almonds, ground

½ cup grated *khoya/mawa*

1 cup yogurt

1 teaspoon white pepper powder

4 tablespoons cream

½ teaspoon green cardamom powder

½ teaspoon rose petal powder

5-6 almonds, slivered

5-6 pistachios, slivered

Edible silver foil

Method

1. Heat the oil in a *handi*; add the onions and sauté till golden brown. Stir in the ginger and garlic pastes.

2. Add the green chilli paste and sauté for five minutes. Add the ground almonds, *khoya* and yogurt. Cook

over low heat for fifteen to twenty minutes.

3. Sprinkle the white pepper powder and mix well.

4. Add the chicken and cook over low heat for another ten minutes, stirring occasionally.

5. Pour in one cup of water and simmer till the chicken is cooked. Stir in the cream.

6. Add the cardamom powder and rose petal powder; simmer for two minutes and remove from heat.

7. Garnish with the edible silver foil, almond and pistachio slivers and serve hot.

Note: For a spicier version, increase the green chilli paste or white pepper powder.

Dalcha

Ingredients

500 grams boneless mutton, cut into
1½-inch pieces

½ cup split Bengal gram, soaked

⅛ cup split green gram, soaked

¼ cup split red lentils, soaked

¾ teaspoon turmeric powder

Salt to taste

2 tablespoons oil

4 green cardamoms

2 black cardamoms

6 cloves

2 one-inch sticks cinnamon

2 medium onions, sliced

1 teaspoon ginger paste

1 teaspoon garlic paste

1 teaspoon coriander powder

3 green chillies, chopped

6-8 roughly torn fresh mint leaves

2 tablespoons chopped fresh coriander

Seasoning

2 tablespoons pure ghee

2 tablespoons tamarind pulp

1 teaspoon cumin seeds

5 garlic cloves, chopped

8-10 curry leaves

½ tablespoon coriander powder

1 teaspoon roasted cumin powder

Method

1. Drain and cook the split Bengal gram, split green gram and split lentils in two cups of water along with one-fourth teaspoon turmeric powder and salt until soft. (The cooked pulses should be completely mashed.)

2. Heat the oil in a *handi;* add the green and black cardamoms, cloves and cinnamon and sauté till fragrant. Add the onions and sauté till golden. Add the ginger paste and garlic paste and sauté for two minutes.

3. Add the mutton, increase the heat and sauté for two or three minutes. Lower the heat, add the coriander powder, remaining turmeric powder and green chillies and sauté for five minutes. Add salt to taste.

4. Add two cups of water and bring the mixture to a boil. Lower the heat and simmer until the mutton is tender. Add the cooked pulses and cook for five minutes until the pulses are well incorporated into the gravy.

5. For the seasoning, heat the ghee in a small pan; add the tamarind pulp, cumin seeds, garlic, curry leaves, coriander powder and cumin powder and sauté over medium heat for two minutes.

6. Add the seasoning to the *dalcha* and cook, covered, for three or four minutes.

7. Serve hot, garnished with mint and coriander.

Mutanjan

Ingredients

1½ cups Basmati rice

500 grams boneless mutton

2 inches ginger

10 garlic cloves

¼ cup ghee

1 medium onion, finely sliced

4 black peppercorns

2 one-inch sticks cinnamon

4 bay leaves

9 green cardamoms

4 black cardamoms

¼ teaspoon grated nutmeg

1 blade of mace

2 tablespoons yogurt, whisked

Salt to taste

1½ cups sugar

2 tablespoons lemon juice

2 tablespoons screw pine essence

2 tablespoons rose water

A few saffron threads

4 cloves

Method

1. Soak the rice in three cups of water for thirty minutes. Drain.

2. Grind half the ginger with five cloves of garlic to a paste. Chop the remaining ginger and garlic finely. Heat the ghee in a pan and sauté the onion till golden brown.

3. Add the peppercorns, one stick of cinnamon, two bay leaves, five green cardamoms, two black cardamoms, the chopped ginger and garlic, nutmeg and mace and continue to sauté for two or three minutes.

4. Add the mutton, yogurt, ginger-garlic paste and salt, and sauté till the ghee separates and the mutton turns golden brown. Add two and a half cups of water, cover and cook till the mutton is tender.

5. Remove the lid and cook till all the water evaporates. Remove the mutton pieces with a slotted spoon and set aside. In a separate pan, cook the sugar and half a cup of water, stirring continuously, till the sugar dissolves to make a thin syrup.

6. Add the lemon juice, one tablespoon each of screw pine essence and rose water. Cover and remove from heat. Soak the saffron in the remaining

screw pine essence and rose water. For the rice, tie the remaining bay leaves, black cardamoms, green cardamoms, cinnamon and cloves in a piece of muslin to make a *potli*.

7. Heat four cups of water in a large pan; add the rice and the *potli*, cover and cook till the rice is half-done. Drain the rice and remove the *potli*.

8. Put the rice back into a *handi*; add the cooked mutton and pour in the sugar syrup, stirring gently to mix well.

9. Sprinkle the saffron, screw pine essence and rose water mixture. Cover and cook on *dum* for thirty minutes. Serve hot.

Ek Handi Nu Dal Bhaat

Ingredients

½ cup split pigeon peas

¾ cup rice

3 tablespoons ghee

½ teaspoon cumin seeds

2-3 cloves

4-5 black peppercorns

1 bay leaf

1 medium onion, sliced

¾ teaspoon ginger paste

¾ teaspoon garlic paste

1 large potato, peeled and cut into 1-inch pieces

¼ teaspoon turmeric powder

¾ teaspoon red chilli powder

¼ teaspoon *garam masala* powder

2 green chillies, chopped

Salt to taste

1 large tomato, puréed

2 tablespoons chopped fresh coriander

Method

1. Heat the ghee in a *handi*; add the cumin seeds, cloves, peppercorns and bay leaf and sauté till fragrant.

2. Add the onion, ginger paste and garlic paste and sauté for one more minute.

3. Add the potato and mix well. Stir in the split pigeon peas and rice.

4. Add the turmeric powder, chilli powder, *garam masala* powder and green chillies and mix well.

5. Add four cups of water and salt. Bring to a boil, lower heat, cover and cook till almost done.

6. Stir in the tomato purée and chopped coriander. Mash the mixture lightly with the back of a ladle.

7. Cook, covered, over low heat for eight to ten minutes and serve.

Methi Makai Biryani

Ingredients

½ cup chopped fresh fenugreek

½ cup corn kernels, boiled

1½ cups Basmati rice, soaked

1 tablespoon oil + for deep-frying

2 medium onions, sliced

1 bay leaf

4 cloves

7-8 black peppercorns

1 black cardamom

¾ cup sour yogurt

Salt to taste

1 teaspoon *garam masala* powder

1 inch ginger, cut into thin strips

2 tablespoons chopped fresh coriander

Masala Paste

2 medium onions, boiled

½ cup grated fresh coconut

1½ inches ginger

4 garlic cloves

1 green chilli

1 teaspoon fennel seeds

1 teaspoon poppy seeds

Method

1. Drain and cook the rice in four cups of water with one teaspoon of oil till done. Drain and set aside.

2. Heat sufficient oil in a *kadai* and deep-fry the sliced onions till brown. Drain on absorbent paper. Grind all the ingredients for the *masala* paste.

3. Heat the remaining oil in a thick-bottomed pan; add the bay leaf, cloves, peppercorns and cardamom and sauté till fragrant. Add the ground paste and sauté till golden brown.

4. Add the yogurt, salt, chopped fenugreek and corn and mix well. Add one cup of water if the mixture is too thick.

5. Spread half the cooked rice in a layer in a *handi* or thick-bottomed pan. Spread half the fenugreek-corn mixture and sprinkle half the *garam masala* powder on top.

6. Repeat the layers once more and top with the browned onions. Cover the pan with aluminium foil and place it on a hot *tawa*. Cook over low heat for about ten minutes.

7. Uncover the pan just before serving and garnish with ginger strips and fresh coriander.

8. Serve hot with *raita* and *papad*.

Lucknowi Murgh Biryani

Ingredients

500 grams chicken on the bone, cut into
   1½-inch pieces
1½ cups Basmati rice, soaked
1 tablespoon ginger paste
1 tablespoon garlic paste
1 teaspoon green chilli paste
1 tablespoon coriander powder
1 tablespoon cumin powder
1 teaspoon *garam masala* powder
1 teaspoon green cardamom powder
Salt to taste
1 cup yogurt
A few saffron threads
1 tablespoon milk

2 tablespoons oil
1 bay leaf
4 cloves
2 green cardamoms
1 black cardamom
5 cups chicken stock
2 tablespoons ghee
1 teaspoon caraway seeds
1 inch ginger, cut into thin strips
¾ cup sliced onions, deep-fried
½ cup chopped fresh mint
2 tablespoons chopped fresh coriander
1 teaspoon screw pine essence
1 teaspoon rose water

Method

1. Marinate the chicken in a mixture of ginger paste, garlic paste, green chilli paste, coriander powder, cumin powder, *garam masala* powder, cardamom powder, salt and yogurt for about half an hour.

2. Soak the saffron in the milk.

3. Heat two tablespoons of oil in a pan; add the bay leaf, cloves, green and black cardamoms, and sauté for half a minute. Add the rice and sauté for one minute. Add the chicken stock and bring to a boil. Lower the heat and cook till the rice is three-fourth done. Drain.

4. Heat the ghee in a *handi* or thick-bottomed pan; add the caraway seeds and sauté for a few seconds. Add the marinated chicken and sauté for three or four minutes, or till half-cooked.

5. Remove the pan from heat. Spread the rice over the chicken. Sprinkle the saffron, ginger strips, fried onions, fresh mint and coriander, screw pine essence and rose water.

6. Cover tightly with a lid and cook on *dum* for fifteen to twenty minutes.

7. Serve hot with *raita*.

Coorgi Mutton Pulao

Ingredients

1½ cups Basmati rice

450 grams mutton on the bone, cut into 1-inch pieces

4 tablespoons ghee

1 medium onion, sliced

Salt to taste

1 tablespoon lemon juice

First Masala

5 garlic cloves

½ inch ginger

2 green chillies

1 tablespoon chopped fresh coriander

5-6 fresh mint leaves

1 small onion

Second Masala

1½ teaspoons coriander seeds

½ teaspoon red chilli powder

3-4 black peppercorns

A pinch of turmeric powder

A pinch of roasted cumin powder

2 cloves

2 green cardamoms

½ inch cinnamon

1½ teaspoons poppy seeds

Method

1. Cook the rice in four cups of water till three-fourth done. Drain and set aside.

2. For the first *masala*, grind the garlic, ginger, green chillies, fresh coriander, mint leaves and onion to a fine paste.

3. For the second *masala*, grind the coriander seeds, chilli powder, peppercorns, turmeric powder, cumin powder, cloves, cardamoms, cinnamon and poppy seeds to a fine paste.

4. Heat the ghee in a *handi* or thick-bottomed pan; add the onion and sauté till golden. Add the first *masala* and sauté for two or three minutes.

5. Add the mutton and sauté for four or five minutes, stirring continuously. Sprinkle some water to prevent scorching.

6. Add the second *masala* and continue to sauté for another two minutes. Add two cups of water and the salt and cook till the mutton is tender and almost dry. Stir in the lemon juice.

7. Add the rice and stir gently to mix. Place the *handi* on a *tawa*, cover and cook on *dum* for twenty to twenty-five minutes. Serve hot.

Mumbai Biryani

Ingredients

1½ cups Basmati rice, soaked

400 grams boneless chicken, cut into
   2-inch pieces

Salt to taste

3 tablespoons oil + for deep-frying

4 large onions, sliced

2 large potatoes, diced

1½ teaspoons garlic paste

2 medium tomatoes, chopped

2 teaspoons roasted cumin powder

2 teaspoons red chilli powder

½ teaspoon turmeric powder

1 inch ginger, cut into thin strips

1 cup yogurt

A few drops of screw pine essence

1 tablespoon *garam masala* powder

Method

1. Drain the rice and cook in four cups
   of water and salt till three-fourth
   done. Drain.

2. Heat sufficient oil in a *kadai;* add three-fourth of the sliced onions and deep-fry till golden. Drain on absorbent paper.

3. Deep-fry the potatoes in the same oil till light brown. Drain on absorbent paper.

4. Heat three tablespoons of oil in a deep *handi;* add the remaining onions and the garlic paste and sauté till lightly browned. Add the tomatoes and cook till the oil separates.

5. Add the chicken, roasted cumin powder, chilli powder and turmeric powder, and sauté for five to six minutes. Add enough water to cover the chicken and simmer till three-fourth done.

6. Add the potatoes, ginger strips, yogurt and salt and cook for another five minutes.

7. Arrange the cooked rice over the chicken pieces. Sprinkle the browned onions, screw pine essence and *garam masala* powder over the rice. Cover with a tight-fitting lid and cook for twenty minutes over medium heat.

8. Serve hot with *raita*.

Handi Biryani

Ingredients

1½ cups rice, soaked and drained

4 medium onions

A few saffron threads

A few drops of screw pine essence

Salt to taste

2-3 green cardamoms

1 black cardamom

2-3 cloves

1 inch cinnamon

1 bay leaf

1 medium carrot, cut into ½-inch cubes

¼ medium cauliflower, separated into small florets

10-15 French beans, cut into ½-inch pieces

½ cup shelled green peas

2 tablespoons oil + for deep-frying

½ teaspoon caraway seeds

½ tablespoon ginger paste

½ tablespoon garlic paste

4-5 green chillies, chopped

1 tablespoon coriander powder

1 teaspoon turmeric powder

1 teaspoon red chilli powder

¾ cup yogurt

2 medium tomatoes, chopped

½ teaspoon *garam masala* powder

2 tablespoons chopped fresh coriander

2 tablespoons chopped fresh mint

2 tablespoons ghee

1 inch ginger, cut into thin strips

Method

1. Chop one onion and slice the rest. Soak the saffron in the screw pine essence.

2. Cook the rice in four cups of boiling salted water with the green cardamoms, black cardamom, cloves, cinnamon and bay leaf, until three-fourth done. Drain and set aside.

3. Mix together the carrot, cauliflower, French beans and peas and boil in three cups of salted water till three-fourth done. Drain and refresh under cold running water. Set aside.

4. Heat plenty of oil in a *kadai* and deep-fry the sliced onions till golden brown. Drain on absorbent paper and set aside.

5. Heat two tablespoons of oil in a thick-bottomed pan and add the caraway seeds. When they begin to change colour, add the chopped onion and sauté until golden brown.

6. Add the ginger paste, garlic paste and green chillies and stir. Add the coriander powder, turmeric powder, chilli powder and yogurt and mix well.

7. Add the tomatoes and cook over medium heat till the oil separates. Add the boiled vegetables and salt and mix well.

8. In a *handi*, arrange alternate layers of cooked vegetables and rice. Sprinkle the saffron-flavoured screw pine essence, *garam masala* powder, chopped coriander and mint, fried onions and ghee in between the layers and on top. Make sure that you end with a rice layer topped with saffron and ginger strips.

9. Cover and seal with aluminium foil or wholewheat flour dough. Place the *handi* on a *tawa* and cook over low heat for twenty minutes. Serve hot with *raita*.

GLOSSARY

ENGLISH	HINDI	ENGLISH	HINDI
Allspice	Kabab chini	Chillies, green	Hari mirch
Almonds	Badam	Cinnamon	Dalchini
Amaranth leaves	Chaulai bhaji	Cloves	Laung
Asafoetida	Hing	Coconut, fresh	Nariyal
Bay leaves	Tez patta	Coconut, dried	Khopra
Bengal gram, split	Chana dal	Coriander seeds	Dhania
Bitter gourd	Karela	Coriander, fresh	Hara dhania
Brinjals	Baingan	Corn kernels	Makai ke dane
Broad beans	Sem/bakla	Cottage cheese	Paneer
Butter	Makkhan	Cottage cheese, creamy	Malai paneer
Capsicum, green	Hari Shimla mirch	Crab	Kekda
Capsicum, red	Lal Shimla mirch	Cream, fresh	Taazi malai
Caraway seeds	Shahi jeera	Cudpah nuts	Chironji
Cardamoms, black	Badi elaichi	Cumin seeds	Jeera
Cardamoms, green	Chhoti elaichi	Curry leaves	Kadhi patta
Carrot	Gajar	Baby corn	Makai
Cashew nuts	Kaju	Edible silver foil	Chandi ka varq
Chicken	Murgh	Egg	Anda
Chicken, boneless	Haddi rahit murgh	Fennel seeds	Saunf
Chillies, dried red	Sookhi lal mirch	Fenugreek seeds	Methi dana

ENGLISH	HINDI	ENGLISH	HINDI
Fenugreek, fresh	Methi bhaji	Peas, dried white	Safed matar
French beans	Farasi	Peppercorns, black	Kali mirch
Garlic	Lehsun	Peppercorns, white	Safed mirch
Ginger, dried	Sonth	Pistachios	Pista
Gram flour	Besan	Pointed gourd	Parwar
Green gram, skinless split	Moong dal	Pomegranate seeds, dried	Anardana
Ladies' fingers	Bhindi	Poppy seeds	Khuskhus
Leg of lamb	Raan	Radish	Mooli
Lemon	Nimbu	Refined flour	Maida
Lentils, red split	Masoor dal	Rice, pressed	Poha
Mace	Javitri	Rose	Gulab
Mango, dried powdered	Amchur	Saffron	Kesar
Millet	Bajra	Sago	Sabudana
Mint	Pudina	Screw pine essence	Kewra jal
Mushroom	Khumb	Shallots	Chhote pyaaz
Mutton	Gosht	Soda bicarbonate	Khane ka soda
Mutton, minced	Keema	Tamarind	Imli
Nutmeg	Jaiphal	Tomatoes	Tamatar
Papaya, unripe green	Papita	Turmeric powder	Haldi
Peanuts, raw	Moongphali	Vinegar	Sirka
Peas, fresh green	Taaze hare matar	Wholewheat flour	Atta
		Yogurt	Dahi